Travel Journal

Enjoy Every Moment!

Keeh Styx

www.gratitudeandmore.ca

Whether you are jet-setting around the globe or enjoying a weekend staycation, this journal will help keep track of your exciting adventures so you remember all of the details.

Fill in the **Places I Want To See** pages and enjoy every moment of your journey getting there.

Do you have more places you dream of seeing? Check out our **Bucket List** journal.

For more information on the wide variety of journals we offer, visit us at www.gratitudeandmore.ca

Have fun!

Leah

Places I Want To See:

1. _____

2. _____

3. _____

4. _____

5. _____

6. _____

7. _____

8. _____

9. _____

10. _____

11. _____

12. _____

13. _____

14. _____

15. _____

Places I Want To See:

16. _____

17. _____

18. _____

19. _____

20. _____

21. _____

22. _____

23. _____

24. _____

25. _____

26. _____

27. _____

28. _____

29. _____

30. _____

Don't Forget to Pack:

The Critical Stuff:
- Clothing
- Passports
- Driver's license
- Credit cards
- Medical insurance card
- Itinerary
- Medications
- Keys
- Camera

Other Important Stuff:
- Cell phone and charger
- Any other electronics
- Emergency contact information
- Snacks and water
- Earplugs

- Headphones
- Books, magazines
- Laundry bag
- Casual clothes
- Dressy clothes
- Sleepwear
- Sweater / Jacket
- Bathing suit
- Shoes
- Sunglasses
- Watch
- Glasses
- Toiletries
- Sunscreen
- Pain reliever
- Vitamins, supplements
- Band-Aids
- This journal

Date: _____ Miles Covered: _____

Start location: _____

Destination: _____

How did I travel: _____

Travelled with: _____

Accommodations: _____

$$ Spent: _____

_____

Adventures Experienced: _____

_____

_____

Meals: _____

_____

What did I miss that I want to come back for: _____

_____

Notes:

_____

_____

_____

_____

_____

_____

_____

_____

_____

_____

_____

Date: _____ Miles Covered: _____

Start location: _____

Destination: _____

How did I travel: _____

Travelled with: _____

Accommodations: _____

$$ Spent: _____

_____

Adventures Experienced: _____

_____

_____

Meals: _____

_____

What did I miss that I want to come back for: _____

_____

Notes:
_____
_____
_____
_____
_____
_____
_____
_____
_____
_____
_____

Date: _____ Miles Covered: _____

Start location: _____

Destination: _____

How did I travel: _____

Travelled with: _____

Accommodations: _____

$$ Spent: _____

_____

Adventures Experienced: _____

_____

_____

Meals: _____

_____

What did I miss that I want to come back for: _____

_____

Notes:

_____

_____

_____

_____

_____

_____

_____

_____

_____

_____

_____

_____

_____

Date: _____ Miles Covered: _____

Start location: _____

Destination: _____

How did I travel: _____

Travelled with: _____

Accommodations: _____

$$ Spent: _____

_____

Adventures Experienced: _____

_____

_____

Meals: _____

_____

What did I miss that I want to come back for: _____

_____

Notes:

_____

_____

_____

_____

_____

_____

_____

_____

_____

_____

_____

_____

_____

Date: _____ Miles Covered: _____

Start location: _____

Destination: _____

How did I travel: _____

Travelled with: _____

Accommodations: _____

$$ Spent: _____

_____

Adventures Experienced: _____

_____

_____

Meals: _____

_____

What did I miss that I want to come back for: _____

_____

Notes:

_____

_____

_____

_____

_____

_____

_____

_____

_____

_____

_____

_____

Date: _____ Miles Covered: _____

Start location: _____

Destination: _____

How did I travel: _____

Travelled with: _____

Accommodations: _____

$$ Spent: _____

_____

Adventures Experienced: _____

_____

_____

Meals: _____

_____

What did I miss that I want to come back for: _____

_____

Notes:

_____

_____

_____

_____

_____

_____

_____

_____

_____

_____

_____

_____

Date: _____ Miles Covered: _____

Start location: _____

Destination: _____

How did I travel: _____

Travelled with: _____

Accommodations: _____

$$ Spent: _____

_____

Adventures Experienced: _____

_____

_____

Meals: _____

_____

What did I miss that I want to come back for: _____

_____

Notes:

Date: _____ Miles Covered: _____

Start location: _____

Destination: _____

How did I travel: _____

Travelled with: _____

Accommodations: _____

$$ Spent: _____

_____

Adventures Experienced: _____

_____

_____

Meals: _____

_____

What did I miss that I want to come back for: _____

_____

Notes:

_____

_____

_____

_____

_____

_____

_____

_____

_____

_____

_____

_____

Date: _____ Miles Covered: _____

Start location: _____

Destination: _____

How did I travel: _____

Travelled with: _____

Accommodations: _____

$$ Spent: _____

_____

Adventures Experienced: _____

_____

_____

Meals: _____

_____

What did I miss that I want to come back for: _____

_____

Notes:

_____

_____

_____

_____

_____

_____

_____

_____

_____

_____

_____

_____

Date: _____ Miles Covered: _____

Start location: _____

Destination: _____

How did I travel: _____

Travelled with: _____

Accommodations: _____

$$ Spent: _____

_____

Adventures Experienced: _____

_____

_____

Meals: _____

_____

What did I miss that I want to come back for: _____

_____

Notes:

_____

_____

_____

_____

_____

_____

_____

_____

_____

_____

_____

_____

Date: _____ Miles Covered: _____

Start location: _____

Destination: _____

How did I travel: _____

Travelled with: _____

Accommodations: _____

$$ Spent: _____

_____

Adventures Experienced: _____

_____

_____

Meals: _____

_____

What did I miss that I want to come back for: _____

_____

Notes:

_____

_____

_____

_____

_____

_____

_____

_____

_____

_____

_____

_____

Date: _____ Miles Covered: _____

Start location: _____

Destination: _____

How did I travel: _____

Travelled with: _____

Accommodations: _____

$$ Spent: _____

_____

Adventures Experienced: _____

_____

_____

Meals: _____

_____

What did I miss that I want to come back for: _____

_____

Notes:

_____

_____

_____

_____

_____

_____

_____

_____

_____

_____

_____

_____

Date: _____ Miles Covered: _____

Start location: _____

Destination: _____

How did I travel: _____

Travelled with: _____

Accommodations: _____

$$ Spent: _____

_____

Adventures Experienced: _____

_____

_____

Meals: _____

_____

What did I miss that I want to come back for: _____

_____

Notes:

Date: _____ Miles Covered: _____

Start location: _____

Destination: _____

How did I travel: _____

Travelled with: _____

Accommodations: _____

$$ Spent: _____

_____

Adventures Experienced: _____

_____

_____

Meals: _____

_____

What did I miss that I want to come back for: _____

_____

Notes:

_____

_____

_____

_____

_____

_____

_____

_____

_____

_____

_____

_____

Date: _____ Miles Covered: _____

Start location: _____

Destination: _____

How did I travel: _____

Travelled with: _____

Accommodations: _____

$$ Spent: _____

_____

Adventures Experienced: _____

_____

_____

Meals: _____

_____

What did I miss that I want to come back for: _____

_____

Notes:

_____

_____

_____

_____

_____

_____

_____

_____

_____

_____

_____

_____

Date: _____ Miles Covered: _____

Start location: _____

Destination: _____

How did I travel: _____

Travelled with: _____

Accommodations: _____

$$ Spent: _____

_____

Adventures Experienced: _____

_____

_____

Meals: _____

_____

What did I miss that I want to come back for: _____

_____

Notes:

_____

_____

_____

_____

_____

_____

_____

_____

_____

_____

_____

_____

Date: _____ Miles Covered: _____

Start location: _____

Destination: _____

How did I travel: _____

Travelled with: _____

Accommodations: _____

$$ Spent: _____

_____

Adventures Experienced: _____

_____

_____

Meals: _____

_____

What did I miss that I want to come back for: _____

_____

Notes:

_____

_____

_____

_____

_____

_____

_____

_____

_____

_____

_____

_____

Date: _____ Miles Covered: _____

Start location: _____

Destination: _____

How did I travel: _____

Travelled with: _____

Accommodations: _____

$$ Spent: _____

_____

Adventures Experienced: _____

_____

_____

Meals: _____

_____

What did I miss that I want to come back for: _____

_____

Notes:

_____

_____

_____

_____

_____

_____

_____

_____

_____

_____

_____

_____

_____

Date: _____ Miles Covered: _____

Start location: _____

Destination: _____

How did I travel: _____

Travelled with: _____

Accommodations: _____

$$ Spent: _____

_____

Adventures Experienced: _____

_____

_____

Meals: _____

_____

What did I miss that I want to come back for: _____

_____

Notes:

_____

_____

_____

_____

_____

_____

_____

_____

_____

_____

_____

_____

Date: _____ Miles Covered: _____

Start location: _____

Destination: _____

How did I travel: _____

Travelled with: _____

Accommodations: _____

$$ Spent: _____

_____

Adventures Experienced: _____

_____

_____

Meals: _____

_____

What did I miss that I want to come back for: _____

_____

Notes:

Date: _____ Miles Covered: _____

Start location: _____

Destination: _____

How did I travel: _____

Travelled with: _____

Accommodations: _____

$$ Spent: _____

_____

Adventures Experienced: _____

_____

_____

Meals: _____

_____

What did I miss that I want to come back for: _____

_____

Notes:

Date: _____ Miles Covered: _____

Start location: _____

Destination: _____

How did I travel: _____

Travelled with: _____

Accommodations: _____

$$ Spent: _____

_____

Adventures Experienced: _____

_____

_____

Meals: _____

_____

What did I miss that I want to come back for: _____

_____

Notes:

Date: _____ Miles Covered: _____

Start location: _____

Destination: _____

How did I travel: _____

Travelled with: _____

Accommodations: _____

$$ Spent: _____

_____

Adventures Experienced: _____

_____

_____

Meals: _____

_____

What did I miss that I want to come back for: _____

_____

Notes:

Date: _____ Miles Covered: _____

Start location: _____

Destination: _____

How did I travel: _____

Travelled with: _____

Accommodations: _____

$$ Spent: _____

_____

Adventures Experienced: _____

_____

_____

Meals: _____

_____

What did I miss that I want to come back for: _____

_____

Notes:

_____

_____

_____

_____

_____

_____

_____

_____

_____

_____

_____

_____

_____

Date: _____ Miles Covered: _____

Start location: _____

Destination: _____

How did I travel: _____

Travelled with: _____

Accommodations: _____

$$ Spent: _____

_____

Adventures Experienced: _____

_____

_____

Meals: _____

_____

What did I miss that I want to come back for: _____

_____

Notes:

Date: _____ Miles Covered: _____

Start location: _____

Destination: _____

How did I travel: _____

Travelled with: _____

Accommodations: _____

$$ Spent: _____

_____

Adventures Experienced: _____

_____

_____

Meals: _____

_____

What did I miss that I want to come back for: _____

_____

Notes:

Date: _____ Miles Covered: _____

Start location: _____

Destination: _____

How did I travel: _____

Travelled with: _____

Accommodations: _____

$$ Spent: _____

_____

Adventures Experienced: _____

_____

_____

Meals: _____

_____

What did I miss that I want to come back for: _____

_____

Notes:

Date: _____ Miles Covered: _____

Start location: _____

Destination: _____

How did I travel: _____

Travelled with: _____

Accommodations: _____

$$ Spent: _____

_____

Adventures Experienced: _____

_____

_____

Meals: _____

_____

What did I miss that I want to come back for: _____

_____

Notes:

_____

_____

_____

_____

_____

_____

_____

_____

_____

_____

_____

Date: _____ Miles Covered: _____

Start location: _____

Destination: _____

How did I travel: _____

Travelled with: _____

Accommodations: _____

$$ Spent: _____

_____

Adventures Experienced: _____

_____

_____

Meals: _____

_____

What did I miss that I want to come back for: _____

_____

Notes:

Date: _____ Miles Covered: _____

Start location: _____

Destination: _____

How did I travel: _____

Travelled with: _____

Accommodations: _____

$$ Spent: _____

_____

Adventures Experienced: _____

_____

_____

Meals: _____

_____

What did I miss that I want to come back for: _____

_____

Notes:

_____

_____

_____

_____

_____

_____

_____

_____

_____

_____

_____

_____

Date: _____ Miles Covered: _____

Start location: _____

Destination: _____

How did I travel: _____

Travelled with: _____

Accommodations: _____

$$ Spent: _____

_____

Adventures Experienced: _____

_____

_____

Meals: _____

_____

What did I miss that I want to come back for: _____

_____

Notes:

Date: _____ Miles Covered: _____

Start location: _____

Destination: _____

How did I travel: _____

Travelled with: _____

Accommodations: _____

$$ Spent: _____

_____

Adventures Experienced: _____

_____

_____

Meals: _____

_____

What did I miss that I want to come back for: _____

_____

Notes:

_____

_____

_____

_____

_____

_____

_____

_____

_____

_____

_____

_____

Date: _____ Miles Covered: _____

Start location: _____

Destination: _____

How did I travel: _____

Travelled with: _____

Accommodations: _____

$$ Spent: _____

_____

Adventures Experienced: _____

_____

_____

Meals: _____

_____

What did I miss that I want to come back for: _____

_____

Notes:

Date: _____ Miles Covered: _____

Start location: _____

Destination: _____

How did I travel: _____

Travelled with: _____

Accommodations: _____

$$ Spent: _____

_____

Adventures Experienced: _____

_____

_____

Meals: _____

_____

What did I miss that I want to come back for: _____

_____

Notes:

Date: _____ Miles Covered: _____

Start location: _____

Destination: _____

How did I travel: _____

Travelled with: _____

Accommodations: _____

$$ Spent: _____

_____

Adventures Experienced: _____

_____

_____

Meals: _____

_____

What did I miss that I want to come back for: _____

_____

Notes:

Date: _____ Miles Covered: _____

Start location: _____

Destination: _____

How did I travel: _____

Travelled with: _____

Accommodations: _____

$$ Spent: _____

_____

Adventures Experienced: _____

_____

_____

Meals: _____

_____

What did I miss that I want to come back for: _____

_____

Notes:

Date: _____ Miles Covered: _____

Start location: _____

Destination: _____

How did I travel: _____

Travelled with: _____

Accommodations: _____

$$ Spent: _____

_____

Adventures Experienced: _____

_____

_____

Meals: _____

_____

What did I miss that I want to come back for: _____

_____

Notes:

_____

_____

_____

_____

_____

_____

_____

_____

_____

_____

_____

_____

52477184R00096

Made in the USA
Charleston, SC
20 February 2016